Kindness to Share from A to Z

Written by Todd & Peggy Snow
Illustrated by Kirsten Sevig

Maren Green Publishing, Inc.
Oak Park Heights, Minnesota

D1416278

To Mom, the kindest person we know.
Love, T.S. and P.S.

• • •

To Alena, Aidan, and Mara for being so kind to me.
K.S.

Ⓜ Maren Green Publishing, Inc.
5525 Memorial Avenue North, Suite 6
Oak Park Heights, MN 55082
Toll-free 800-287-1512

Library of Congress Publication-in-data is available.

Edited by Pamela Espeland
Text set in Adobe Garamond Pro and Futura
Illustrations created using a crow quill pen, India ink, and
watercolor on Fabriano paper

First Edition November 2008
10 9 8 7 6 5 4 3 2 1
Manufactured in China

ISBN 978-1-934277-16-4 (pbk.)

www.marengreen.com

Kindness is for sharing
in what you say and do.
Being kind is good for others
and how you should be treated, too.

Ask someone to play with you.

Bring flowers to a person who needs cheering up.

Collect canned food for people who are hungry.

Food Drive

Do something nice for another person just because.

Entertain the younger kids at a family party.

Forgive someone
who makes a mistake.

Give someone a compliment.

Help clean up after dinner.

Invite the new kid at school to sit with you at lunch.

Join a good cause.

Kiss your parents goodnight.

Listen when others are talking.

Make cookies to welcome new neighbors.

Notice when someone is kind to you. Say "Thank you."

Offer to help without waiting to be asked.

Pick up after yourself.

Quiet down when others are trying to sleep.

Read a story to a younger child.

Say
"I love you."

Think before you speak.
Choose kind words.

Use other people's things with care.
Ask first.

Wait your turn.

eXplain how to play a game
so others can join in.

Yell good things at a game,
like "Yay!" and
"Go team go!"

Zip a younger child's jacket.